Essential Quest
Why are rules important?

MW00682328

Government
RULES

by Anton Wilson

Chapter 1
Rules Protect Us

The government makes rules to keep people safe.

Rules can be very helpful! They help people get along. They help us stay safe. When we all follow rules, people know what to expect. This can make life better.

Our country's government has rules. They help you and your family every day. Some rules protect public places. Some keep our food and medicines safe. Some protect nature and animals. And some protect people's ideas.

People who visit Yellowstone National Park can see this geyser known as "Old Faithful."

National Parks

Have you ever visited a national park? National parks are open to everyone. The world's first national park was Yellowstone National Park. It was founded in the United States in 1872. Mountains, rivers, lakes, and forests form this park.

This sign lets people know the park is a protected place.

Today, there are almost 400 national park sites in the United States. Some are places of natural beauty, such as the Grand Canyon. Others are important to our history. The Statue of Liberty is one of these parks. The National Park Service has rules. It protects these places. It makes sure people follow the rules. That way everyone will be able to enjoy national parks for many years to come.

Chapter 2
Food Rules

The USDA stamp lets you know this meat is safe to eat.

Did you know rules help keep your food safe? The United States Department of Agriculture (USDA) checks certain foods. These include meat, chicken, and eggs. The USDA makes sure these foods are safe to eat. They must be free of disease. Look at foods in the grocery store. You'll see the USDA stamp on some packages.

It is important to eat a good breakfast and lunch to help you learn at school.

School Lunches

The USDA also makes rules that affect food you eat in school. Many schools provide meals to students. Schools that follow USDA rules get extra food and money. This helps them provide breakfasts and lunches. Students may eat for free. Others can buy low-cost meals.

Food Safety

The USDA has fact sheets with rules. These help people handle and prepare foods safely. For example, some foods must be cooked to a certain temperature. Following food safety rules can save lives!

Before cooking meat or chicken, people read the Safe Handling Instructions on the package.

Image Source/Getty Images

How to Store Eggs Safely

Type of egg	Can be refrigerated for	Can be frozen for
raw egg	3–5 weeks (in shell)	I year (out of shell)
hard-boiled egg	I week	do not freeze
store-bought eggnog	3–5 days	6 months

The government gives us information about how to store and serve food safely. Did you ever wonder how long certain foods can be kept in the refrigerator? The government provides this information. It tells what temperature certain foods, such as meats, must reach before they can be safely eaten.

Medicines

Government rules affect medicine, too. Drugstores sell medicines to help sick people get better. The Food and Drug Administration (FDA) tests these drugs. It looks for possible unpleasant **side effects**. It checks to see how much of the medicine people should take. Finally, after a lot of testing, the FDA may **approve** a drug. Then it can be prescribed or sold.

The FDA has guides to help people understand the rules for taking medicines.

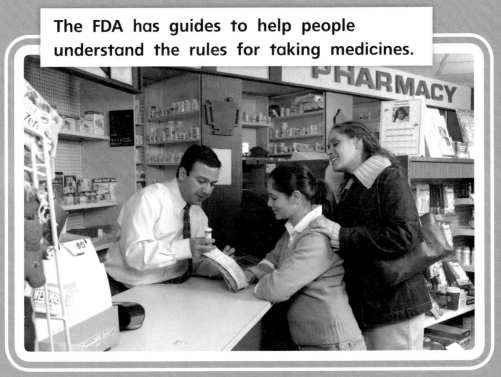

Chapter 3

Animal Rules

The U.S. Fish and Wildlife Service protects hundreds of animal species. These include endangered fish, bats, bears, and foxes.

The United States is home to animals and plants. They are protected by the government. The government makes rules about hunting and fishing. People must get a written **permit** for these activities. If they are caught hunting or fishing without a permit, they must pay a fine.

Photodisc Collection/Getty Images

The Florida Everglades are home to many animal and plant species.

The U.S. Fish and Wildlife Service also protects animals' habitats. People need a permit to boat or camp in certain swamps. They have to obey rules. This way, they do not harm the area's plants and animals. Even people who own land must follow rules about its use. For example, people cannot build new homes on or near wetlands. They must follow this rule even if they own the land.

11

Chapter 4
Idea Rules

To find a book's copyright page, look at the page right after the title page.

Government rules protect people's ideas. Writers, artists, and others are protected.

Look inside any book. You will find a **copyright** page. Copyright rules say that no one can copy and sell a published book without permission. When the author first exclaimed, "I have an idea!" he or she probably wasn't thinking about copyright. But these rules protect writers.

Famous Names in Patents

- Alexander Graham Bell: telephone
- John Deere: steel plow
- Orville and Wilbur Wright: airplane
- John Kellogg: breakfast cereal

cereal

Patents

Other rules protect inventions. The U.S. Patent and Trademark Office helps protect the rights of people who invent something new. An inventor can get a patent. This is a paper that says the inventor owns his or her invention.

Many products in your home have patents.

Suppose you invented something new, like a toy. You would not want others to copy your idea! It is your invention. You should be able to make money from it. A patent protects inventors. It says no one can make, use, or sell the invention without the inventor's permission.

Government rules help improve our lives. They protect our health and safety. They protect our rights. By following rules, you can help make our world a better place.

Respond to Reading

Summarize

Use details to help you summarize *Government Rules.*

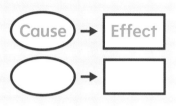

Text Evidence

1. How do you know *Government Rules* is expository text? Genre

2. What caused the government to create rules about food? Cause and Effect

3. Use what you know of multiple-meaning words to tell the meaning of *fine* on page 10. Multiple-Meaning Words

4. Why is it important to have rules that protect national parks? Text to World

Compare Texts
Read about why pool rules are important.

POOL RULES

Pools are fun places to swim. Some pools are outside. Some pools are inside. Pools are different. But most of them have the same rules.

Pool rules are easy to find. Most pools have big signs posted where everyone can see them. Sometimes, rules are all on one big sign. Some pool signs use symbols. These catch people's attention.

Many cities have public pools.

Diving

Some pools have a deep end. Other pools are not deep enough for diving. Diving in shallow water is unsafe. People could hit their heads on the pool bottom. "No Diving" rules keep people safe.

Running

People must walk carefully around a pool. Running near a pool is dangerous. A person could slip on the wet deck and fall. People can break an arm or a leg this way. That's why the "No Running" sign is important.

Eating and Drinking

Usually people may not eat or drink in the pool area. Dropping food or drinks in the pool makes the water dirty. People can slip on food left on the deck. Glass drink bottles might break.

Bare feet and broken glass don't go together! This is why many pools have special areas where you can get a snack or drink.

You can have fun *and* stay safe at the pool. Just follow the rules!

 Make Connections
What is one important rule you follow?
Essential Question
What are three ways rules help keep you safe? Text to Text

Glossary

approve *(uh-PROOV)* to judge a thing acceptable or good *(page 9)*

copyright *(KOP-ee-right)* owning something that you wrote so you can make money from it *(page 12)*

permit *(PUR-mit)* a written note that allows someone to do something *(page 10)*

side effects *(SIGHD uh-fekts)* ways a medicine affects the body besides its main effects *(page 9)*

Focus on
Social Studies

Purpose To find out why classroom rules are important

What to Do

Step 1 List at least three rules in your classroom.

Step 2 Write the three rules in the first column of a chart like this one.

Rule	How It Helps

Step 3 In the second column, write one way each rule helps you and your class.

Step 4 Talk about what you learned.